tourism TATTLER

Issue 01 (JANUARY) 2016

PUBLISHER
Tourism Tattler (Pty) Ltd.
PO Box 891, Umhlanga Rocks, 4320
KwaZulu-Natal, South Africa.
Website: _www.tourismtattler.com_

EXECUTIVE EDITOR Des Langkilde
Cell: +27 (0)82 374 7260
Fax: +27 (0)86 651 8080
E-mail: _editor@tourismtattler.com_
Skype: tourismtattler

MAGAZINE ADVERTISING
ADVERTISING DIRECTOR Bev Langkilde
Cell: +27 (0)71 224 9971
Fax: +27 (0)86 656 3860
E-mail: _bev@tourismtattler.com_
Skype: bevtourismtattler

SUBSCRIPTIONS
http://eepurl.com/bocldD

BACK ISSUES (Click on the covers below).

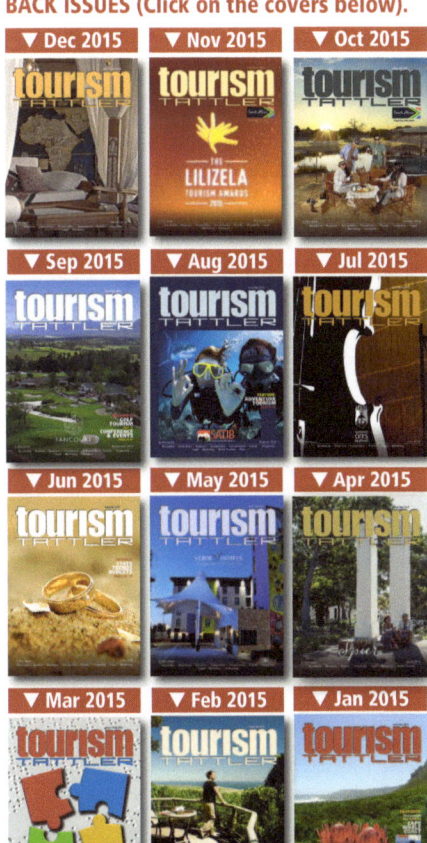

▼ Dec 2015	▼ Nov 2015	▼ Oct 2015
▼ Sep 2015	▼ Aug 2015	▼ Jul 2015
▼ Jun 2015	▼ May 2015	▼ Apr 2015
▼ Mar 2015	▼ Feb 2015	▼ Jan 2015

Contents

13 BUSINESS: Super-rich Tourism in Africa.

24 MARKETING: Hotel Industry Trends for 2016.

26 RISK: Understanding Tourism Insurance.

IN THIS ISSUE

EDITORIAL CONTRIBUTORS

Adv. Louis Nel   Anne Briggs   Martin Janse van Vuuren
Andrew Macfarlane   Marlien Lourens   Michelle Mangan

MAGAZINE SPONSORS

08 Amakosi Safari Lodge   09 ADGE Apartment Hotel
08 Arinara Bangtao Beach Resort   09 Gondwana Game Reserve

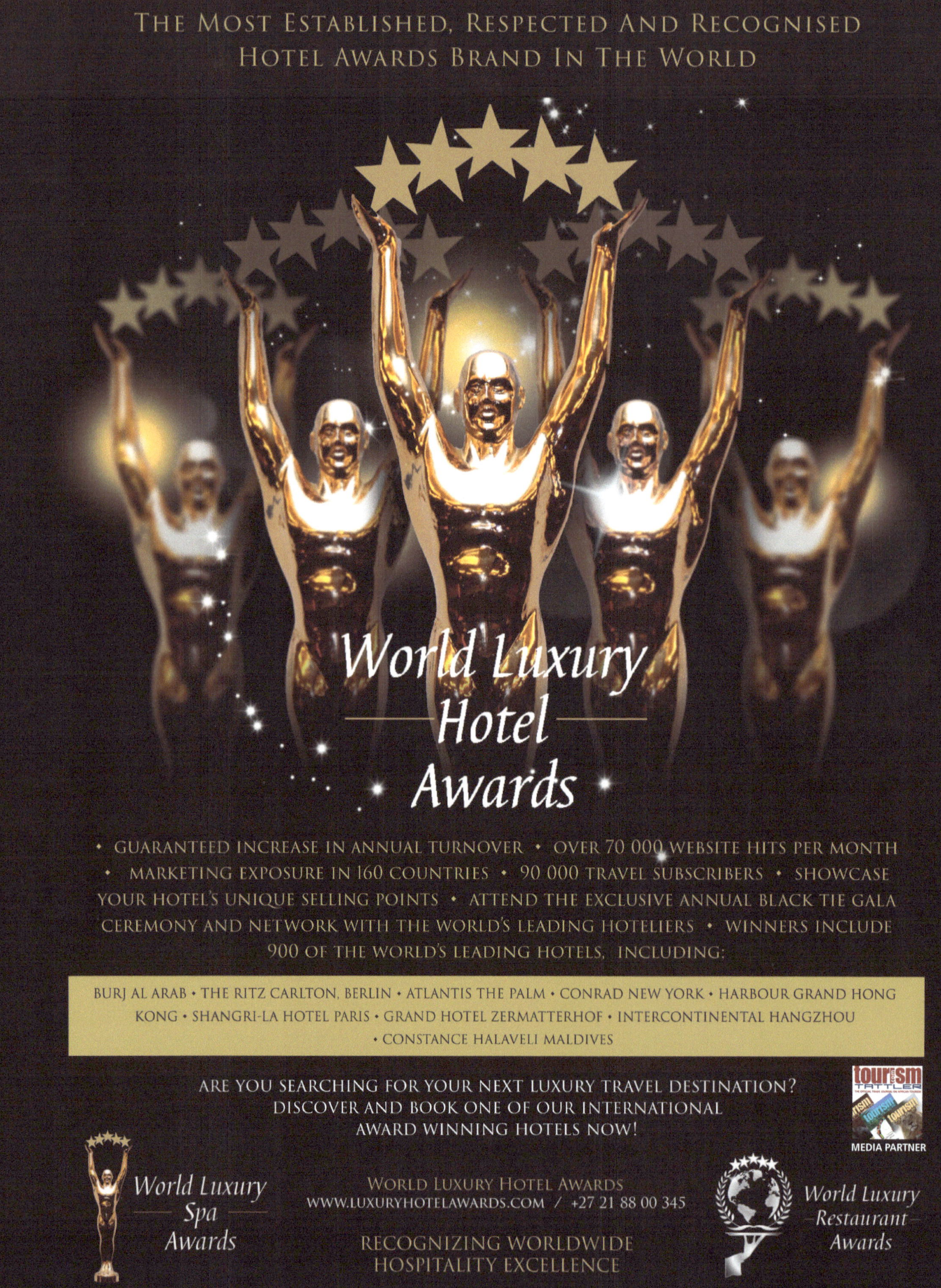

THE MOST ESTABLISHED, RESPECTED AND RECOGNISED
HOTEL AWARDS BRAND IN THE WORLD
World Luxury Hotel Awards
• GUARANTEED INCREASE IN ANNUAL TURNOVER • OVER 70 000 WEBSITE HITS PER MONTH • MARKETING EXPOSURE IN 160 COUNTRIES • 90 000 TRAVEL SUBSCRIBERS • SHOWCASE YOUR HOTEL'S UNIQUE SELLING POINTS • ATTEND THE EXCLUSIVE ANNUAL BLACK TIE GALA CEREMONY AND NETWORK WITH THE WORLD'S LEADING HOTELIERS • WINNERS INCLUDE 900 OF THE WORLD'S LEADING HOTELS, INCLUDING:
BURJ AL ARAB • THE RITZ CARLTON, BERLIN • ATLANTIS THE PALM • CONRAD NEW YORK • HARBOUR GRAND HONG KONG • SHANGRI-LA HOTEL PARIS • GRAND HOTEL ZERMATTERHOF • INTERCONTINENTAL HANGZHOU • CONSTANCE HALAVELI MALDIVES
ARE YOU SEARCHING FOR YOUR NEXT LUXURY TRAVEL DESTINATION?
DISCOVER AND BOOK ONE OF OUR INTERNATIONAL
AWARD WINNING HOTELS NOW!
tourism TATTLER
MEDIA PARTNER
World Luxury Spa Awards
WORLD LUXURY HOTEL AWARDS
WWW.LUXURYHOTELAWARDS.COM / +27 21 88 00 345
RECOGNIZING WORLDWIDE
HOSPITALITY EXCELLENCE
World Luxury Restaurant Awards

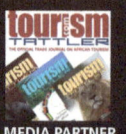

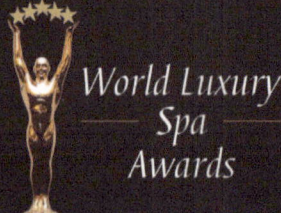

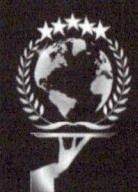

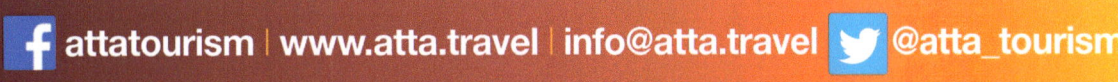

Accreditation

The Africa Travel Association (ATA)

Tel: +1 212 447 1357 • Email: info@africatravelassociation.org • Website: www.africatravelassociation.org

ATA is a division of the Corporate Council on Africa (CCA), and a registered non-profit trade association in the USA, with headquarters in Washington, DC and chapters around the world. ATA is dedicated to promoting travel and tourism to Africa and strengthening intra-Africa partnerships. Established in 1975, ATA provides services to both the public and private sectors of the industry.

The African Travel & Tourism Association (Atta)

Tel: +44 20 7937 4408 • Email: info@atta.travel • Website: www.atta.travel

Members in 22 African countries and 37 worldwide use Atta to: Network and collaborate with peers in African tourism; Grow their online presence with a branded profile; Ask and answer specialist questions and give advice; and Attend key industry events.

National Accommodation Association of South Africa (NAA-SA)

Tel: +2786 186 2272 • Fax: +2786 225 9858 • Website: www.naa-sa.co.za

The NAA-SA is a network of mainly smaller accommodation providers around South Africa – from B&Bs in country towns offering comfortable personal service to luxurious boutique city lodges with those extra special touches – you're sure to find a suitable place, and at the same time feel confident that your stay at an NAA-SA member's establishment will meet your requirements.

Regional Tourism Organisation of Southern Africa (RETOSA)

Tel: +2711 315 2420/1 • Fax: +2711 315 2422 • Website: www.retosa.co.za

RETOSA is a Southern African Development Community (SADC) institution responsible for tourism growth and development. RETOSA's aims are to increase tourist arrivals to the region through. RETOSA Member States are Angola, Botswana, DR Congo, Lesotho, Madagascar, Malawi, Mauritius, Mozambique, Namibia, Seychelles, South Africa, Swaziland, Tanzania, Zambia and Zimbabwe.

Southern Africa Tourism Services Association (SATSA)

Tel: +2786 127 2872 • Fax: +2711 886 755 • Website: www.satsa.com

SATSA is a credibility accreditation body representing the private sector of the inbound tourism industry. SATSA members are Bonded thus providing a financial guarantee against advance deposits held in the event of the involuntary liquidation. SATSA represents: Transport providers, Tour Operators, DMC's, Accommodation Suppliers, Tour Brokers, Adventure Tourism Providers, Business Tourism Providers and Allied Tourism Services providers.

Southern African Vehicle Rental and Leasing Association (SAVRALA)

Contact: manager@savrala.co.za • Website: w

Founded in the 1970's, SAVRALA is the representative voice of Southern Africa's vehicle rental, leasing and fleet management sector. Our members have a combined national footprint with more than 600 branches countrywide. SAVRALA are instrumental in steering industry standards and continuously strive to protect both their members' interests, and those of the public, and are therefore widely respected within corporate and government sectors.

Seychelles Hospitality & Tourism Association (SHTA)

Tel: +248 432 5560 • Fax: +248 422 5718 • Website: www.shta.sc

The Seychelles Hospitality and Tourism Association was created in 2002 when the Seychelles Hotel Association merged with the Seychelles Hotel and Guesthouse Association. SHTA's primary focus is to unite all Seychelles tourism industry stakeholders under one association in order to be better prepared to defend the interest of the industry and its sustainability as the pillar of the country's economy.

International Coalition of Tourism Partners (ICTP)

Website: www.tourismpartners.org

ICTP is a travel and tourism coalition of global destinations committed to Quality Services and Green Growth.

International Institute for Peace through Tourism

Website: www.iipt.org

IIPT is dedicated to fostering tourism initiatives that contribute to international understanding and cooperation.

World Travel Market

WTM Africa - Cape Town in April, WTM Latin America - São Paulo in April, and WTM - London in November. WTM is the place to do business.

World Youth Student and Educational (WYSE) Travel Confederation

Website: www.wysetc.org

WYSE is a global not-for-profit membership organisation.

The Safari Awards

Website: www.safariawards.com

Safari Award finalists are amongst the top 3% in Africa and the winners are unquestionably the best.

World Luxury Hotel Awards

Website: www.luxuryhotelawards.com

World Luxury Hotel Awards is an international company that provides award recognition to the best hotels from all over the world.

Our January 2016 cover shows an image of the universe – an appropriate metaphor for the 2015 Luxury Hotel Awards winners – each of whom have attained stardom in their respective fields of recognition (*see our Accolades story on pages 07 to 09*).

The stars have always been a source of wonder to mankind. Think of it this way: You are one of billions of people on our Earth; our Earth orbits the Sun in our Solar System; our Sun is one star among the billions in the Milky Way Galaxy; and our Milky Way Galaxy is one among the billions of galaxies in our Universe, which makes you unique in the Universe! And what better place to view the Milky Way Galaxy than in Africa.

Coming back to planet Earth, there's no denying that the travel and tourism industry worldwide has experienced challenges over the past year. The tougher global economic climate has seen tourists curtail travel plans, take longer to decide on a holiday destination, and when they do, they book at the last minute. All of which makes forward planning for the travel trade a lot tougher.

Ms Sthembiso Dlamini, the Acting CEO at South African Tourism summed it up in her New Year message: "As we look ahead to 2016, we are hopeful and optimistic about what the year holds. Despite challenges that may arise, we remain very hopeful that our allure as a destination will continue to draw people to South Africa.

"I invite you to join us and complement our global and regional marketing initiatives by continuing to deliver on the ground what we promise the world: A destination that is scenically beautiful, exceptional service standards of our industry, and tourism infrastructure matched only by the warm welcome of our people.

"I implore you too to support us also by participating at our Trade Shows, INDABA and Meetings Africa. Preparations for Africa's biggest leisure and business tourism trade shows are already in full swing and all indications are that we are well on track to host successful shows."

Speaking of trade shows, in this edition we feature the ASEAN Tourism Forum 2016, to which Tourism Tattler has been invited as hosted media (*see page 19*).

We look at the global hotel industry and trends for 2016 (*page 24*), provide seven steps for successful route tourism development (*page 14*), and feature the best route west through the Northern Cape (*page 10*).

Ahead of International Tourist Guides Day, which will be celebrated on 18 February 2016, we have a feature on Tourist Guiding in South Africa (*page 20*), and start an in-depth series on Understanding Tourism Insurance (*page 26*).

And finally, an encouraging report from Mpumalanga Tour Operators who are *gatvol* with Traffic Officer Bribery (*page 17*).

Enjoy your reading and do let us have your thoughts and comments.

Des Langkilde.
editor@tourismtattler.com

*Published with acknowledgement to **Zapiro** and **Mail & Guardian**.*

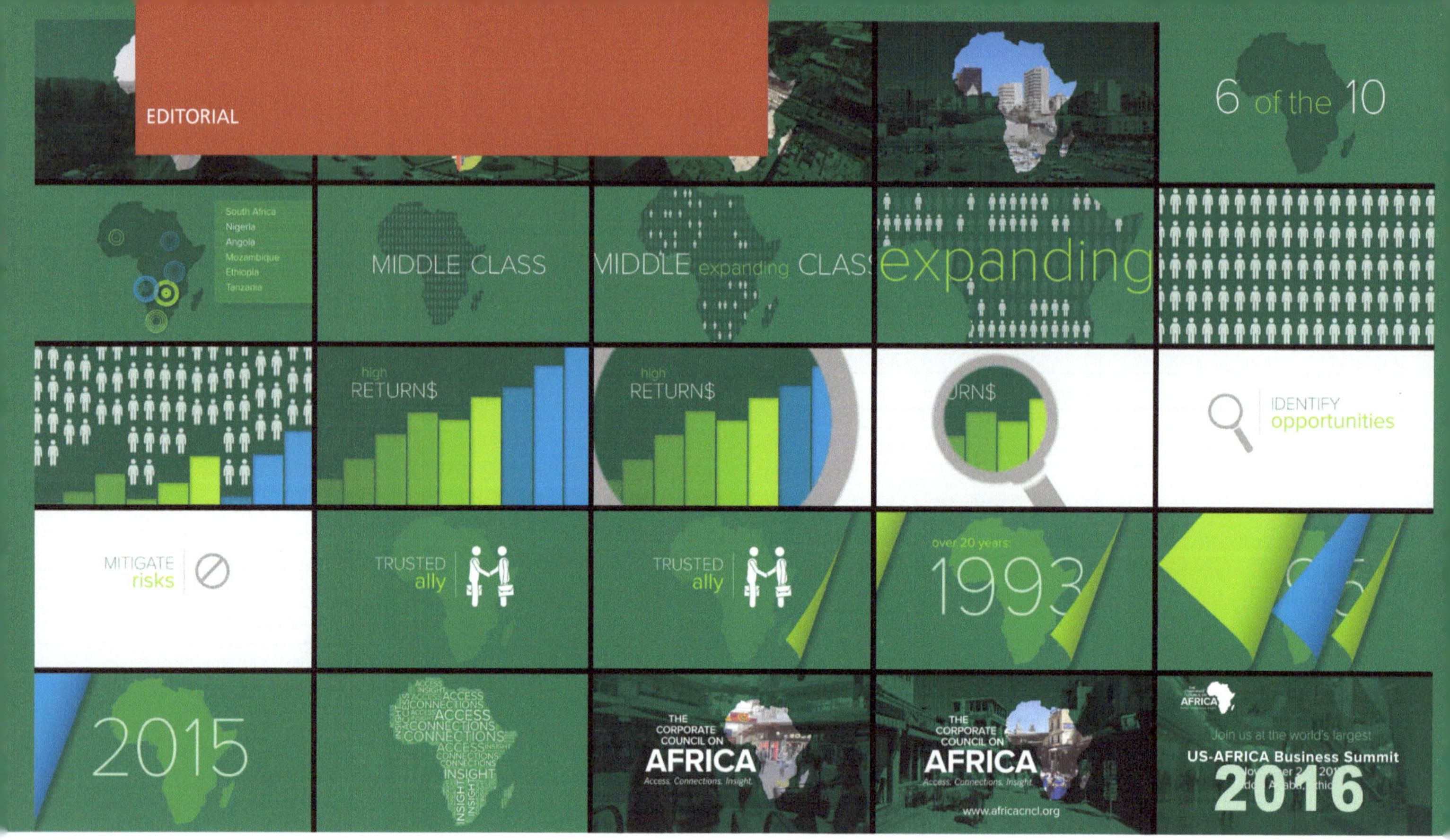

South Africa
Nigeria
Angola
Mozambique
Ethiopia
Tanzania

MIDDLE CLASS

MIDDLE expanding CLASS

expanding

high RETURN$

high RETURN$

RN$

IDENTIFY opportunities

MITIGATE risks ⊘

TRUSTED ally

TRUSTED ally

over 20 years: 1993

2015

ACCESS CONNECTIONS INSIGHT

THE CORPORATE COUNCIL ON AFRICA. Access. Connections. Insight.

THE CORPORATE COUNCIL ON AFRICA. Access. Connections. Insight.

Join us at the world's largest US-AFRICA Business Summit 2016
www.africacncl.org

ATA adopted by CCA

Officially announced at the New York Times Travel Show on January 8, 2016, the Africa Travel Association (ATA) will become an operating element under the Corporate Council on Africa (CCA).

The ATA is America's oldest travel organization dedicated to US-Africa tourism since 1975 and long considered the top global organization promoting tourism to Africa

Stephen Hayes, President and CEO of the CCA said, "The addition of the Africa Travel Association (ATA) to our portfolio of activities strengthens both the Africa Travel Association and the Corporate Council on Africa. Tourism is an essential ingredient in growing the economies of Africa. The potential for growth and investment in tourism in nearly every country in Africa is simply huge, regardless of the stage of development."

The opportunity to combine the two organization presented itself when long-time ATA Executive Director, Edward Bergman, announced he would step down from his position at the end of 2015, following the successful ATA 40th Annual World Congress in Nairobi, Kenya this past November (*read Tourism Tattlers report* here).

Edward Bergman added "Finding a home for the Africa Travel Association at the Council provides an opportunity for the travel industry within Africa and between the United States and the countries of Africa to reach new heights. The Corporate Council's focus on investment and development matches the requirements of today and supplements ATA's existing cultural and historic tourism endeavors throughout Africa. It was hard to imagine a better match for both organizations."

CCA has been a leading advocate for US-Africa trade and investment since its founding in 1993 through a grant from then Secretary of Commerce Ron Brown and the United States Agency for International Development. In the past 23 years, the council has grown to incorporate one hundred eighty corporations representing approximately eighty-five percent of all US private investment in

Africa. CCA focuses on various sectors for investment including infrastructure, financing, health, energy, power, and agribusiness.

Mr. Hayes added, "Our background in working with major corporate players and investors who are looking for new opportunities in Africa is a perfect fit for the historical mission of the ATA for driving tourism growth on the African continent beyond its current global market share of this three percent of international travel."

ATA will operate in Washington, DC as a division of the Corporate Council on Africa.

For more information visit www.africacncl.org *and* www.africatravelassociation.org

World Luxury Hotel Awards

Hotels in Australia, South Africa, and Thailand fared well at the the 9th Annual World Luxury Hotel Awards, which was hosted at the prestigious Harbour Grand Hong Kong on Saturday 24th October 2015.

And the winner is...

Hosted by international television presenter, Desmond So, over 300 attendees represented their hotels to receive their awards at this red carpet, black tie event. The phenomenal success of this event echoes in the praise of the attendees who, not only celebrated their accomplishments and received their awards on an international stage, but also enjoyed stellar presentation, a delectable 6 course fine dining experience and sensational cultural performances in the extravagant and glamourous Grand Ballroom at the **Harbour Grand Hong Kong** (*read Tourism Tattler's article here*).

200 winners, in over 50 categories received their awards at the event. The Overall Winner was announced at the climax of the event. New York's Hotel Plaza Athénée was awarded the Overall Winner Award. The award was presented by Mr Brandon Lourens, founder and chairman of the World Luxury Hotel Awards, as well as Ms. Odile Franc, Director of Distribution and Development, France 24.

In the Luxury Serviced Apartments category, Australia's **ADGE Apartment Hotel** in Sydney took the coveted award as the Worlds Best. The ADGE Apartment has been recognised for its unique design and strong focus on quality guest service.

Arinara Bangtao Beach Resort, which overlooks the sapphire sea on the west coast of Phuket, Thailand won the Worlds Best Luxury Coastal Resort category award. This family friendly resort is recognised for its signature Southeast Asian décor and special features such as direct pool access, stunning pool and sea views and spacious living areas.

South Africa also fared well at the 2015 World Luxury Hotel Awards. **Gondwana Game Reserve**, situated in the heart of the Eastern Cape's Garden Route, won the Worlds Best Luxury Eco Safari Resort award. This 11,000-hectare (26,000 acre) Private Game Park offers a distinctive and luxurious malaria-free Safari Holiday destination with free-roaming Big 5 Safari Animals.

The Worlds Best Luxury Bush Lodge award went to **Amakhosi Safari Lodge**. Located on the banks of Zululand's Mkuze River in KwaZulu-Natal, Amakhosi Safari Lodge offers 6 luxury River Suites and launched the new Amakhosi River SPA in November 2013 with a range of signature Africology treatments.

The 2015 awards season saw the introduction of the Chairman's Award which is awarded to hotel management companies that have earned the respect of their peers in the travel industry and travelers alike. The first ever Chairman's Award was awarded to LUX* Hotels and Resorts, Mauritius, for maintaining the highest standards in the management of the Lux* group, through the experienced leadership of master hoteliers, combined with vigilance in the delivery of excellent service. This award recognizes the Lux* management group for sustaining the highest standards of hospitality and luxury, as a common thread, throughout the various hotels and resorts in their portfolio.

To enter the 2016 World Luxury Hotel Awards register at www.luxuryhotelawards.com

The Harbour Grand Hong Kong's Grand Ballroom with crystal chandeliers - host venue to the 2015 World Luxury Hotel Awards Gala Ceremony.

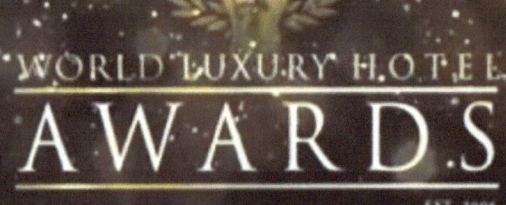

The best route west through the Northern Cape

The legendary highway Route 66 in the United States conjures up images in traveller's mind of the open road and adventure. Everyone dreams of taking a road trip through new landscapes, visiting strange destinations, and cruising towards the horizon. South Africa has equally majestic roads to travel along, and one that is becoming increasingly popular is the N14, writes **Andrew Macfarlane**.

Starting in Pretoria, Gauteng, the road travels through the North West province, into the Northern Cape and ends in Springbok - a two hour drive from the ocean. Roughly 1186 kilometres in length, and a 12-hour drive, the majority of the highway is in the country's largest province, which (fun fact) is larger in size than Germany. As you head through the Highveld, Kalahari, and the Richtersveld, the scenery changes dramatically throughout the journey.

But before any long road trip can take place you need to plan. With the road passing through towns, some nature reserves, and areas where animals cross the highway freely, it's a good idea to take some time to rest and take in the scenery. Here are five stop-over points on the best road to chase the setting sun across South Africa:

Baberspan Bird Sanctuary

Situated in the North West province just outside the small town of Delareyville, the Baberspan Bird Sanctuary is a great stop-over spot. The reserve has over 365 species of birds and is one of the largest waterfowl sanctuaries in South Africa. Travellers can make a trip to the park into an overnight stay. There are multiple accommodation options including camping along the shoreline of the dam where you can do a spot of fishing, set up your caravan, or book yourself into one of the guesthouses (the Flamingo or Pelican house). The Baberspan Bird Sanctuary is 200 hectares of pristine bird watching paradise.

The Dream Lodge

When travelling through the sun-baked Kalahari, it's a good idea to head towards the oasis - in this part of the world that's Kuruman. The town was established in this region due to the natural underground spring, the Eye of Kuruman. The N14 runs straight through the centre of the town and a great stop-over spot is the Dream Lodge. Recently opened by professional motivational speaker and life coach Godfrey Madanhire, the venue caters to multiple workshops and seminars on a wide range of topics. Spending the day at this destination will leave you refreshed and with a new set of life skills. Up the road from the lodge is the Moffat Mission Station, steeped in history it has been frequented by none other than legendary explorer Sir David Livingston.

The African Vineyard Guest House

Just 25 kilometres outside the centre of Upington, this island resort is something different from other locations on your journey through the Kalahari. Situated on an island in the middle of the Orange River (the largest river in South Africa), the African Vineyard is a bit of opulence that you'll welcome on your journey across the Northern Cape. Surrounded by grape and fruit orchards, it is an easy hour's drive from Augrabies Falls. With wine tasting, game drives, and river rafting on the itinerary list for the area, this is something completely different from what most South Africans expect from the Kalahari.

▼ *A flamboyance of flamingo at Barberspan Bird Sanctuary.*

▲ *An aerial view of the Orange River Delta in Upington area.*
▼ *Vinyards at the African Vineyard Guesthouse in Upington,*

All images courtesy of Northern Cape Tourism Authority

▲ *Early morning canoeists enjoy the tranquil serenity of the Orange River as it winds beneath the N14 bridge through Upington.*

▼ *Moffat Mission Station in Kururman.*

Annie's Cottage

Located right in the centre of Springbok at the foot of the *Koppie*, South Africa's first copper mine, this is a true home away from home. Annie's Cottage is an old manor house that has been painstakingly restored to its former beauty. It is a great hop-off point to take in the sights and sounds of the Namaqualand. The area is graced with an awesome flower show like no other from August to October when hills are covered with brightly-coloured flora. The N14 officially ends in Springbok, but then again it's very close to the ocean if you wish to make your journey just that little bit longer.

Scotia Inn Hotel

The small seaside town of Port Nolloth is a remote and charming destination, as well as an easy two-hour journey via the R355 from Springbok. Established as a port for copper exports, and eventually diamonds, the town's commercial days have subsided. If you've travelled straight across the country (as per the directions of this guide) you'll want to be right on the beachfront. The Scotia Inn is situated right on the coast, with an uninterrupted view of the beautiful Atlantic Ocean. Expect to wake up to majestic misty mornings as the winds from the ocean meet the warm desert air close to the Namibian border. But, best of all, you can enjoy the sunsets on a pristine beach – you've earned it after chasing the sun across the countries biggest province.

▲ *Fun on the beach at Port Nolloth.*
▼ *The Richtersveld landscape.*

SATSA
Southern Africa Tourism
Services Association

Grant Thornton

B✓NDED*

Market Intelligence Report

The information below was extracted from data available as at **07 January 2016**. By **Martin Jansen van Vuuren** of **Grant Thornton**.

ARRIVALS

The latest available data from **Statistics South Africa** is for **January to September 2015***:

	Current period	Change over same period last year
UK	282 301	-0.1%
Germany	162 714	-9.7%
USA	218 585	-7.5%
India	58 373	-12.3%
China (incl Hong Kong)	56 412	-19.7%
Overseas Arrivals	1 481 296	-8.4%
African Arrivals	4 997 522	-6.4%
Total Foreign Arrivals	6 488 114	-6.9%

HOTEL STATS

The latest available data from **STR Global** is for **January** to **September 2015**:

Current period	Average Room Occupancy (ARO)	Average Room Rate (ARR)	Revenue Per Available Room (RevPAR)
All Hotels in SA	61.9%	R 1 057	R 654
All 5-star hotels in SA	61.3%	R 1 901	R 1 166
All 4-star hotels in SA	60.9%	R 1 000	R 609
All 3-star hotels in SA	62.0%	R 861	R 533
Change over same period last year			
All Hotels in SA	0.9%	5.9%	6.9%
All 5-star hotels in SA	0.3%	8.2%	8.5%
All 4-star hotels in SA	1.8%	5.2%	7.1%
All 3-star hotels in SA	-0.8%	6.2%	5.3%

ACSA DATA

The latest available data from **ACSA** is for **January to November 2015**:

Change over same period last year	Passengers arriving on International Flights	Passengers arriving on Regional Flights	Passengers arriving on Domestic Flights
OR Tambo International	0.1%	-2.1%	9.6%
Cape Town International	9.5%	8.8%	8.4%
King Shaka International	-5.9%	N/A	6.0%

CAR RENTAL DATA

The latest available data from **SAVRALA** is for **January to June 2015**:

	Current period	Change over same period last year
Industry rental days	8 139 127	-1%
Industry utilisation	70.2%	-0.7%
Industry Average daily revenue	2 498 944 728	1%

WHAT THIS MEANS FOR MY BUSINESS

Foreign tourism continues to decline (see Statistics South Africa data) while domestic tourism remains positive (see passengers arriving on domestic flights). It is hoped that the changes to the visa regulations will be implemented soon in order for foreign tourism numbers to recover. *Note that African Arrivals plus Overseas Arrivals do not add to Total Foreign Arrivals due to the exclusion of unspecified arrivals, which could not be allocated to either African or Overseas. As from January 2014, Stats SA has stopped counting people transiting through SA as tourists. As a result of the revision, in order to compare the 2014 figures with 2013, it is necessary to deduct the transit figures from the 2013 totals.*

For more information contact Martin at Grant Thornton on +27 (0)21 417 8838 or visit: http://www.gt.co.za

Super-rich Tourism in Africa

A recent study by New World Wealth titled 'Millionaire Tourism in Africa', says that around 43,000 multi-millionaires visited Africa in the 12 months to September 2015.

South Africa was the most popular African destination for the super-rich, with roughly 11,000 multimillionaires visiting the country during the 12 month period.

The report adds, "This was despite new visa rules that made it more difficult for visitors to go to South Africa."

Africa has always been a destination for the super-rich. The study drills down into the continent's relationship with the Ultra High Net Worth community and has come up with a series of findings as to where the upper wealthy go, and in what numbers.

Major destinations for the super-rich within South Africa included: Cape Town, Johannesburg, Umhlanga, Franschoek, Stellenbosch, and Kruger Park (mainly around Sabi Sands) and the Garden Route (mainly around Knysna).

According to the study, Chinese and Indian millionaires are common visitors to Africa, especially to South Africa, Seychelles, Mauritius and Kenya.

Outside of South Africa, major destinations for international millionaires included: Mauritius, Seychelles, Marrakech in Morocco, Casablanca in Morocco, Cairo in Egypt, Nairobi in Kenya, the Serengeti in Tanzania, Sharm El Sheikh in Egypt, the Masai Mara in Kenya, Livingstone in Zambia and the Okavango Swamps in Botswana. Gorilla safaris in Bwindi Forest (Uganda) and in the Virunga Mountains are also popular.

There is a slight shift in movement, however, with the Chinese and Indian rich. Chinese and Indian millionaires used to visit Morocco and Egypt a lot a few years back but seem to no longer be going there in big numbers. This may be due to the recent rise in religious violence in these countries.

The second most popular African country for the super-rich to visit, according to the latest report, is Morocco with 4,000 such visitors, followed by Botswana (3,000), Kenya (3,000), the Seychelles (3,000), Tanzania (2,000), Egypt (2,000), Mauritius (2,000), Uganda (1,000), Zambia (1,000), Mozambique (1,000) and Nigeria (1,000).

The numbers of general multi-millionaire visitors to African countries, rounded to the nearest thousand, are broken down as follows.

Country visitors

South Africa	11 000	Morocco	4 000	Botswana	3 000
Kenya	3 000	Seychelles	3 000	Tanzania	2 000
Egypt	2 000	Mauritius	2 000	Uganda	1 000
Zambia	1 000	Mozambique	1 000	Nigeria	1 000

The report also rated the top safari lodges in Africa that the super rich prefer.

Favorite Safari Lodges
- Ngorongoro Crater Lodge Ngorongoro, Tanzania
- Ngala Tented Camp Timbavati, SA
- Savanna Sabi Sands, SA
- Royal Livingstone Livingstone, Zambia
- Londolozi Sabi Sands, SA
- Cottar's 1920s Safari Camp Masai Mara, Kenya
- Nxabega Tented Camp Okavango Delta, Botswana
- Singita Ebony Lodge Sabi Sands, SA
- Sanctuary Gorilla Forest Camp Bwindi, Uganda
- Savute Elephant Lodge Chobe, Botswana

The top rated small boutique hotels (with less than 30 rooms) are listed below. Lodges are excluded. The study points out that three of them are located in the town of Franschoek.

Best Boutique Hotels
- La Petite Dauphine Franschoek, SA
- North Island Seychelles
- Franschoek Country House Franschoek, SA
- Cleopatra Natal Midlands, SA
- La Residence Franschoek, SA

The top rated normal sized hotels in Africa are listed below.
- La Mamounia Marrakech, Morocco
- 12 Apostles Hotel & Spa Cape Town, SA
- Royal Mansour Marrakech, Morocco
- Hemingways Nairobi, Kenya
- The Oyster Box Umhlanga, SA
- Lost City and Sun City North West, SA
- Four Seasons Sharm El Sheikh, Egypt
- Cape Grace Cape Town, SA
- Beverley Hills Hotel Umhlanga, SA
- 10 Four Seasons Seychelles.

Another study by New World Wealth titled 'Top African cities for millionaires' states that there are approximately 163,000 millionaires living in Africa (as of June 2015), with combined wealth holdings of US$670 billion. Note: 'Millionaires' refer to individuals with net assets of US$1 million or more.

Johannesburg is the top African city for millionaires. There are also sizable millionaire populations living in Cairo, Lagos and Cape Town.

The 'Top African cities for millionaires' report can be downloaded *here*.

7 Steps to Successful Route Tourism Development

The following article is an edited extract from a Master of Tourism degree dissertation by **Marlien Lourens**, and is as valid today as it was when first drafted in 2007.

Some observers describe the notion of 'route development' as the world's best hope to secure sustainability in travel and tourism. The concept of tourism routes refers to an *"initiative to bring together a variety of activities and attractions under a unified theme and thus stimulate entrepreneurial opportunity through the development of ancillary products and services"*. Route tourism is thus a market-driven approach for tourism destination development.

In several parts of the world, the concept of rural trails or heritage routes has been used, particularly in the context of promoting rural tourism. Routes seem to be a particularly good opportunity for the development of less mature areas with high cultural resources that appeal to special interest tourists, who often, not only stay longer, but also spend more to pursue their particular interest. Routes appeal to a great variety of users such as overnight visitors that visit the route as part of a special interest holiday, or day visitors that frequent the route (or part of it) on excursions. The essential concept of route tourism is simple, namely that of the linking together a series of tourism attractions in order to promote local tourism by encouraging visitors to travel from one location to another.

The development of tourism routes offers opportunities for the formation of local development partnerships. Some of the best and most successful examples of such 'rural routes' are the development of wine or food circuits, which have been widely researched in Europe, North America and Australasia.

In South Africa, considerable activity also surrounds the development of 'route tourism', involving a linkage together of the tourism resources of a number of smaller centres and collectively marketing them as a single tourism destination region. For many South African small towns, route tourism is a vital component of local economic development. The development of wine routes as part of the strong and growing interest in special interest, wine tourism represents one of the most well-known examples.

Tourism is an important economic sector in Africa within more than half of Sub-Saharan Africa countries. The possibilities of tourism are of growing interest to governments and donor organisations in respect of poverty alleviation. Indeed it is regarded significant that the South African Government's Trade and Industry Chamber, through its Fund for Research into Industrial Development, Growth and Equity (FRIDGE) commissioned the development of a strategic plan for routes and community-based tourism in 2005 (ECI Africa, 2006).

In common with the international experience, in South Africa it can be argued that there are considerable research gaps regarding the changing nature of the market for routes tourism, the needs and motivations of visitor markets, awareness of tourism routes and whether visitors rate touring routes as attractions in their own right or as a means to reach an end destination. In addition, best practice on route tourism development and marketing experience from both overseas and South Africa is not being documented or shared between local stakeholders.

Steps to successful route tourism development

At the outset it must be recognised that most destinations involved in route tourism in South Africa are emerging destinations. It is evident that these destinations need guidelines to assist them through their development phases. The developmental phases of routes have been identified as establishment and positioning, growth and maturity, as graphically portrayed in Figure 5.1. The various phases of development as shown in Figure 5.1 are recognised by specific characteristics. Each phase and its characteristics are described below.

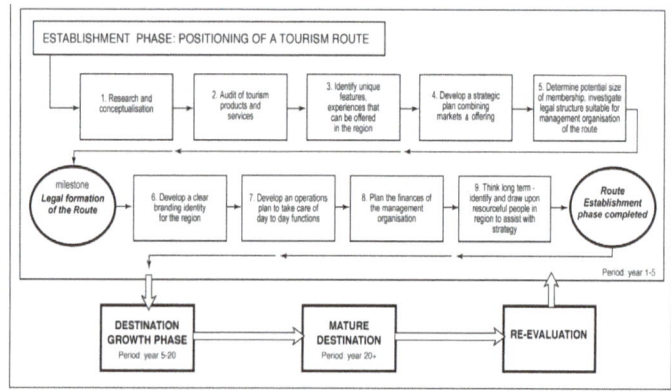

Figure 5.1: Process of Establishing and Positioning of a Route Tourism Destination

When a new route destination is developed, it is usually unrecognised in the market place with only a small number of visitors to the area and limited tourism infrastructure. During this phase committed leadership is required to see the potential and develop a vision for the region. The establishment and conceptualisation phase of a route as shown in Figure 5.1 contains nine steps, which could take between one and five years to complete. Precision and inclusiveness

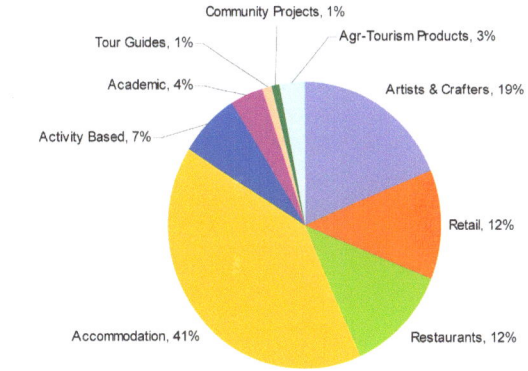

Image courtecy of Mercedes-Benz Commercial Vehicles

are required during the establishment and conceptualisation phase to ensure the desired long-term effects.

Firstly, the route must be conceptualised based on solid market research, which identifies key target markets and their requirements. Market research must be conducted on a continuous basis to ensure that the latest tourism trends are included into objectives and strategies for the area. When budgets are tight, it is necessary to align the destination to a local, regional or provincial tourism authority or link to a local university to provide students or volunteers to assist with market research.

Secondly, an audit of tourism products within the designated area must be conducted. This audit may include the natural environment, man-made products and human assets.

Assessments of existing product must be conducted to ensure that products are keeping up to date with the changing dynamics of the tourism industry. The association must clearly determine a minimum standard (equal or higher than the national grading system) for members and a system for regular re-assessment. Failing to set minimum standards, might jeopardise tourist experiences in the area and cause negative marketing which, in the long run, may result in unsuccessful destinations.

Unique selling features

The third step is to scrutinise the tourism assets and identify the unique selling features or experiences of the area and its products. Unique features are extremely important to distinguish and position the destination in the market place. Once the unique selling features have been identified, a macro level strategic plan must be conducted that combines the market requirements and the tourism assets of the region, providing a consolidated approach towards the future development of the area. It is important that the area consults its local, regional and provincial authorities regarding its strategy and future plans for the area. This will ensure that the envisaged route coincides with the macro planning for the region and potentially could link with broader planning or funding initiatives.

The next step will be to determine the potential size of the possible membership base.

Tourism products with the ability to complement the unique features and main themes of the route must be lobbied to join the organisation from the early stages. If a legal structure is not yet in place, legal advice must be sought on the best structure suitable for any potential management organisation. Once the organisation is formed, specific portfolios for committee members must be developed according to the identified strategic objectives and to ensure nominated members have the willingness and experience to perform within these portfolios.

Mentorship

It is advisable to incorporate mentorship within the committee and sub-committees or task teams for sustainability of skills. Care must be taken not to incorporate products that are not complementary to tourism or the envisioned branding and values of the area for revenue gain. The association should avoid putting dominant members who act for personal or political gain into management positions. It is also important to be inclusive of all stakeholders within the region to ensure that the benefits are shared by all members of the community.

Further, destination managers should encourage product diversification in the area by putting systems in place to incentivise the correct product mix for the area. For example, it is not healthy for an area to have only accommodation establishments. Accordingly, an association in an area with many accommodation establishments should have high joining fees for products falling within this category. Research conducted as part of this study shows the importance of unique attractions in a destination and how these products could be used as draw-cards to induce the use of support services. As shown in the analysis of the Midlands Meander graph below, special events can also be used to produce the same effect.

Breakdown of tourism products in the Midlans Meander (2006)

After the membership plan is finalised, the association must determine and plan a clear brand identity for the region. The importance of marketing the destination according to its identity, determined by its unique features must be stressed. Marketing in the form of public relations is more affordable and sometimes more effective than hard core marketing, especially in the case of emerging destinations. The misrepresentation of the destination in marketing material can be fatal to the reputation of a destination, it is crucial not to overstate and under-deliver.

When marketing a destination it is important to know which market is targeted and what its key requirements are. As shown in the case studies, it is likely that the largest proportion of the market for a route will be locals from within a region. It is thus essential that proper signage of a route, according to the chosen branding, should be one of the first marketing actions to perform. The signage and branding of the region is important for the development of public awareness and acknowledgement.

The next step must be to determine a clear strategy to direct the work plan and day to day operations of the organisation. This requires an operations plan that ensures good communication between the association and its members as well as the roles and responsibilities of committee members and staff. In this way the association avoids the danger of fragmentation between committee members and other members.

Finances

The planning of finances is crucial for the overall survival of an association. Initially it is important to allocate resources according to strategic importance. The association and its members must constantly remind themselves to think on a long-term basis especially as most projects start small and can take 20 to 30 years to mature and deliver substantial economic benefits. The association must therefore be realistic about its setting goals for itself in the short term. Nonetheless, it is advisable to work towards the appointment of full-time staff for the achievement of faster results.

Once the establishment and conceptualisation phase has been complete, the destinations enter a growth phase. This phase is characterised by increasing visitation levels that attract local investment in tourism and public investment in infrastructure. The destination and market share come into being with the efforts of advertising and marketing. As demonstrated in the local and international case studies, the management focus should be to implement a good product development strategy which could lead to growth in visitor demand. The growth phase is usually extended over a long period of time. It starts in year five of a destination and could last until year twenty from the inception of the route.

Re-evaluation

From year twenty onwards, destinations usually reach maturity. This phase is characterized by the fact that the main income of the local economy comes from tourism and the visitation levels continue to increase albeit at a decreasing rate. As was demonstrated by the analysis of the Midlands Meander this phase exemplifies extensive efforts in advertising and marketing to overcome the seasonality and to develop new markets. During maturity, the importance of tourism is appreciated fully by the local population. At this stage, a wide range of markets are attracted and the growth rate is slowing down. Management efforts during maturity should be focused on the maintenance of markets and quality of visitor experiences; especially during peak season when capacity limits are reached. When maturity is reached it may happen that markets start perceiving the route destination as "unfashionable". At this point, it might be necessary for destination managers to re-evaluate the position of the area and revisit the steps in the establishment phase to prevent the route from falling into stagnation.

Although the focus of the planning guidelines is biased towards private sector-driven development, these guidelines can also be used by public sector planners. The private sector driven approach has proven to be more practical and successful in the southern African environment. Ultimately the institutional structure for a successful destination demands an effective partnership between the public and private sector organisations responsible for tourism within a particular destination. Certain functions, such as macro planning, are better suited to the public sector. Design and implementation of funded programmes to complement macro planning initiatives is a function that should reside within the public sector and is extremely important for the success of destination development initiatives.

The full dissertation document, as submitted by Marlien Lourens to the University of the Witwatersrand, School of Geography, Archaeology and Environmental Studies may be downloaded here.

Seven steps for successful tourism routes

Step 1: The route must be grounded in solid market research that identifies key target markets and their needs - this must be done on an ongoing basis to be responsive to trends and shifts in markets.

Step 2: An audit should be done on the tourism products in the area including all natural and cultural assets. It may be valuable to determine criteria to be included as part of the route to ensure consistency of quality in the travel experience.

Step 3: Scrutinize the assets to determine the unique selling features of the area and then develop a macro level strategic plan to consolidate tourism planning for the area.

Step 4: Determine the size of the membership base for suppliers on the route - the buy in of these members is critical to the success of the route for they are the ultimate delivery agents of the experience. It is important to ensure the product mix is diverse and does not over represent any of the sectors (i.e. accommodations) as visitors will expect that all aspects of their experience will be available.

Step 5: Members should establish a clear brand identity for the route and then market this according to the targets identified.

Step 6: Members should decide upon what sort of governance and operational structure they need to ensure that the route is maintained.

Step 7: Members should think long term about the finances required to make the route a success in the minds of visitors. The author suggests that many routes start small and can take 20-30 years to mature and deliver substantial economic benefits and therefore realistic goals should be set about return on investment.

Tour Operators Oppose Traffic Officer Bribery

SATSA and KLT have taken steps to reduce inappropriate fines levied against tourists and tour operators by traffic officers in the South African province of Mpumalanga, writes **Anne Briggs**.

Last year, the Southern Africa Tourism Services Association (SATSA) Mpumalanga Chapter and Kruger Lowveld Tourism (KLT) got together with a very small delegation of very senior South African Police Services (SAPS) and traffic department officials. There were just five of us and let's just say that the two and half hours of discussions were 'lively' – at times I became very lively indeed! – but by the end of the meeting we had reached agreement on a number of new approaches to counter inappropriate fines and we have some great plans.

The traffic department is now as determined as we are to return us to the corruption-free calm that we enjoyed in January 2015 (when we had six weeks without a single case of a bribe demanded from a tourist). They have a print-out of my 35 page dossier of corruption cases with areas highlighted where there is sufficient information for follow-up.

We have also implored them to appreciate that it is not for us to educate tourists not to pay bribes – it is for them to ensure that their officers don't ask for them. I pointed out that in every other civilised country, if you offered a traffic officer a bribe, he would arrest you for trying to bribe him, whereas in South Africa it is the traffic officers who are asking for bribes and the tourists who are resisting!

From our side – and to back up the process of personally addressing all the traffic officers of the Ehlanzeni district, in which we are actively involved – we have agreed to step up once again the information we give to our tourists. So please, to make your maximum contribution, be absolutely sure that every single client that you meet receives an anti-corruption card and an explanation of what to do in the event that they are stopped and asked for cash. We have to stamp this out. We are receiving more and more reports of clients who won't come back here and tour operators who are avoiding our area.

We shall also be phoning in reports of cases detailed enough to follow up, but we will only be able to do this when we have chase-able facts like vehicle number-plates and officers' names. The best thing the client can do is to absolutely insist on being given a written fine on the requisite form, just as we South Africans would, because that contains all the details we need. They can then send us the fine, tell us how much the suggested bribe was and we can follow up with the officers concerned. Only that way will we identify the individuals and let them know that we are onto them, day after day, until they give up.

Remember that, whatever you might have heard, it is illegal to photograph someone without their permission. SAPS are adamant on that one.

So, another 100 000 anti-corruption cards were printed by KLT at their expense for us to distribute. We must inform tourists, we must put suggestions into our guest information packs, and we must help to find the names/numbers of the culprits. In return, we have a good rapport with traffic and SAPS who now understand the gravity of the situation and have various plans (joint and several) as to how they (and we) are going to attack the problem. This has to be a co-operative effort and we have to believe it will work. And we must do everything to forewarn our guests, without alarming them. We shall continue to pressurise the car hire companies too. And we are pursuing one case through the courts, thanks to input from The Lowvelder, Barberton and Graskop.

Let's flood the market with the cards, and we shall also be flooding the traffic police with the cards at our briefings. SAPS will also hand them out.

There is no room for negativity here. I am hopeful, but we must keep up the pressure. It is my absolute priority. Every time I hear of a corrupt act by a traffic officer, I take it personally, so determined am I to wipe this out. And we have to get back the 'normality' of not having to warn tourists, because there should be no risk of corruption. That is how things should be.

If you have evidence of bribery by traffic officers in the Mpumalanga province email me at _tours@mfafa.co.za_

Read more on this subject:
South Africa's Traffic Officers Damaging Tourism

About the author: Anne Briggs is the presiding SATSA Mpumalanga Chapter Chair and owner of Mfafa Tours.

Competition

'Like' / 'Share' / 'Connect' with these Social Media icons to win!

The winning 'Like' or 'Share' during the month of **January 2016** will receive a
6-cup (800ml) Chrome Coffee Maker with the compliments of **Livingstones Supply Co** – *Suppliers of the Finest Products to the Hospitality Industry*.

Livingston Supply Company

Tourism Tattler

Competition Rules: Only one winner will be selected each month on a random selection draw basis. The prize winner will be notified via social media. The prize will be delivered by the sponsor to the winners postal address within South Africa. Should the winner reside outside of South Africa, delivery charges may be applicable. The prize may not be exchanged for cash.

Congratulations to our December Social Media winner

Winner

@LuckyBucketSA   @blazeitzn

Marc McDonald has been selected as our **December 2015** winner for his 'Follow & Tweet' on **Twitter**. Marc will receive a **6-cup (800ml) Chrome Coffee Maker** with the compliments of **Livingstones Supply Co** – *Suppliers of the Finest Products to the Hospitality Industry*.

For more information visit www.livingstonessupplyco.com

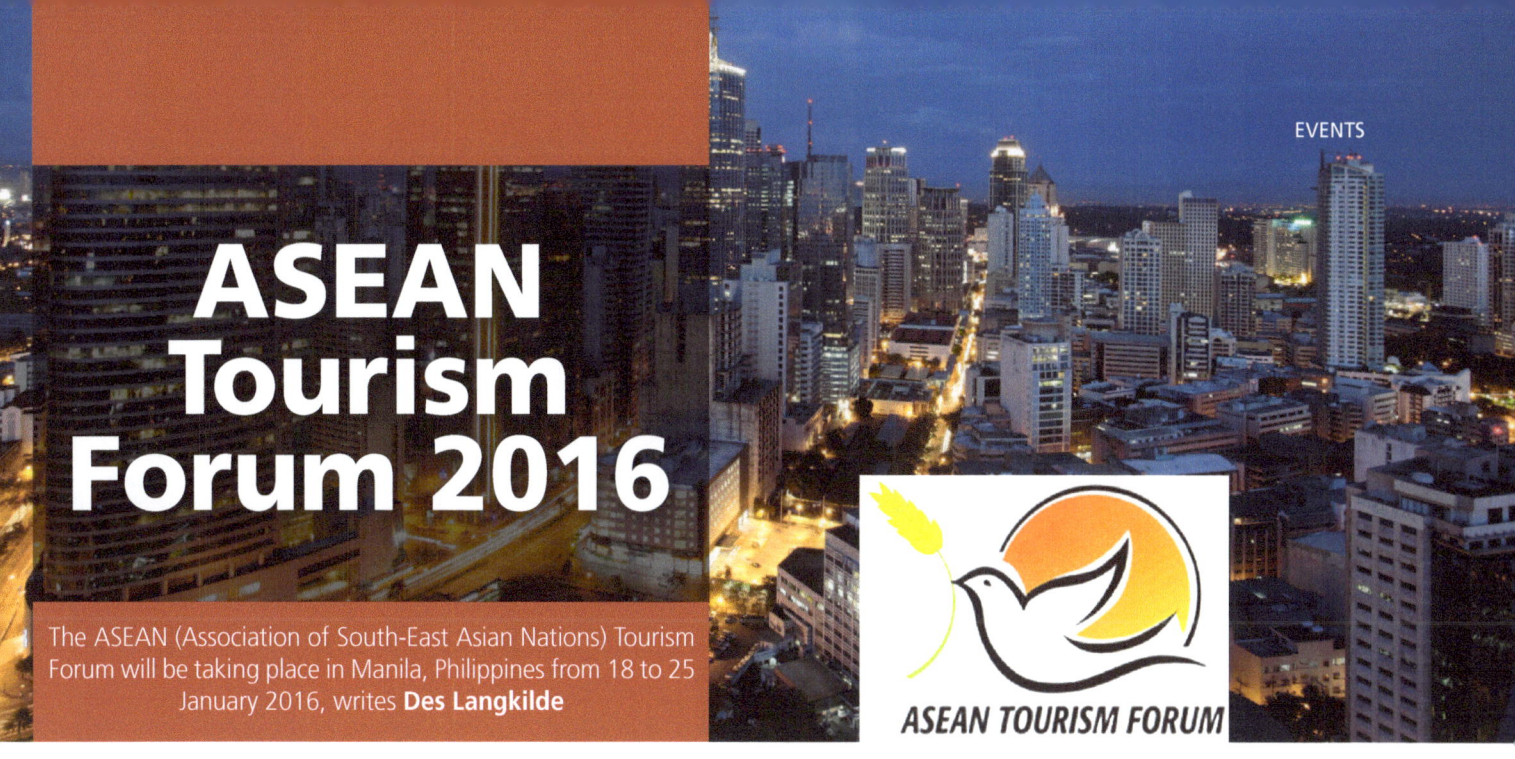

ASEAN Tourism Forum 2016

The ASEAN (Association of South-East Asian Nations) Tourism Forum will be taking place in Manila, Philippines from 18 to 25 January 2016, writes **Des Langkilde**

ASEAN TOURISM FORUM

According the World Travel & Tourism Council's latest report on the Philippines (The Economic Impact of Travel & Tourism 2015), the direct contribution of Travel & Tourism to GDP was PHP533.0bn (4.2% of total GDP) in 2014, and was forecast to rise by 4.9% in 2015, and to rise by 5.6% pa, from 2015-2025, to PHP964.0bn (4.4% of total GDP) in 2025. Visitor exports generated PHP255.7bn (6.9% of total exports) in 2014, and is forecast to grow by 6.6% pa, from 2015-2025, to PHP485.2bn in 2025 (9.9% of total).

Considering the importance of Travel and Tourism to the Philippines economy, the Government of the Philippines has enhanced its mechanisms and collaborations with various agencies to bolster the country's tourism offering. It has made massive investments in infrastructure, from constructing and rehabilitating roads and highways to tourism clusters and tourism destination areas, including the upgrading of airports and seaport.

One such collaboration is the ASEAN (Association of South-East Asian Nations) Tourism Forum (ATF), a cooperative effort that aims to promote the ASEAN region as a single tourist destination. ATF is an annual gathering that brings together the member countries of the ASEAN to discuss innovations, trends, and developments in the tourism industry and facilitate joint policy formulations to accelerate the growth of the region's tourism.

"Most people describe the countries in our region as 'fiercely competitive', but upon closer inspection one realizes that the more the countries of ASEAN compete, the more that we all tend to gravitate towards growth. Our region is characterized by competition – a cooperative, collaborative decision by all players to compete with each other so that the world will choose the region before choosing the country. Our countries become, in very real terms, each other's value extension – we become each other's developing markets. And to make this development last for our children, we have to make certain that we are mindful of the social and environmental context that our region's growth exists in," says Ramon R. Jimenez, Jr, the Philippines Secretary of Tourism.

The theme for ATF 2016 is 'One Community For Sustainability', which embodies unity in diversity and is a colourful and vibrant tropical 10-in-one paradise like no other. Its great outdoors and rich culture unique to each country, bands the 10-member nations as one regional destination in tourism.

"The Philippines Department of Tourism is honoured and proud to host ATF 2016. With this theme, the 35th edition of the forum will launch the new ASEAN Tourism Strategic Plan (ATSP) 2016 – 2020, which will work towards not only the development and growth of the region's tourism, but also in ensuring that this growth is grounded on responsible, sustainable, and inclusive tourism.

We welcome all ATF 2016 delegates to our home and hope that you will experience our country in different ways — from our diverse natural wonders to our rich cultural heritage and the warmth of the Filipino people. And while this forum will allow for the exchange of ideas for the progress of our economies, we also hope that these meetings will build stronger friendships between our nations," concludes Jimenez.

With tourism being a vital foothold in the economic and social growth of the region and its countries, ASEAN is committed to strive towards delivering a quality destination experience for each and every visitor, an endeavour that is centred on responsibility, sustainability and inclusive tourism development.

With the 10-member states collaborating and striving towards sustainable tourism, the star that is South-East Asia promises to shine bright as the destinations achieve a flourishing balance of growth and preservation, a formula that will benefit the local population and elevate poverty.

The beauty of South-East Asia lies in its enchanting DNA of warm and hospitable people, culture, language, religion, architecture, cuisine and geography, where old centuries meet the 21st century. ASEAN has since captivated every spectrum of today's traveller – from adventure seekers, backpackers, businessmen, families, to photography enthusiasts, those seeking sun, sand and sea, trekkers, and more.

Whether for business or for pleasure, South-east Asia wants to continue maintaining a high level of tourist satisfaction, ensuring a meaningful experience to its tourists while raising their awareness about sustainability issues and promoting sustainable tourism practices amongst them.

To capture a piece of the past, to take advantage of the present, and to secure a return in the future to relive the wondrous experience all over again – ASEAN seeks to realise its tourism ambitions with sustainability that respects the local people, the traveller, its cultural heritage and the environment.

For more information or to register visit www.atf2016.com

How to Become a Tourist Guide

International Tourist Guides Day will be celebrated on 18 February 2016, and ahead of this event we investigate how to become a tourist guide in South Africa, what makes a good tourist guide, and how and where they find work.

Who is a Tourist Guide?

Any person who, for monetary or other reward, accompanies people who are travelling through or visiting any place within a country, and who furnishes those people with information or comments concerning a place or objects visited is defined as a Tourist Guide. Many tourist guides may also wish to run their own tour operations in which they are both tour guide and tour operator.

Categories of tourist guides

There are three categories of tourist guides:
Site Guides – these tourist guides have attained the minimum qualification in order to guide in a "limited geographical area" i.e. Hiking in the Drakensberg, visiting the Natal Battlefields, taking a day tour of Cape Town, visiting Soweto;
Provincial Guides – are qualified to take tourists around an entire province i.e. Limpopo or Gauteng;
National Guides – are permitted to conduct tours around South Africa, crossing all provincial boundaries. These guides would accompany people taking a comprehensive tour of South Africa, say, by coach.

Classification of Tourist Guides

Adventure Guides – conduct a guided adventure experience e.g. rock climbing, paddling, abseiling, etc.

Nature Guides – conduct a guided natural experience in areas such as Game Reserves, National Parks, nature conservation areas, trails, and the like.

Cultural Guides – conduct a guided cultural experience in a limited geographical area such as a museum, community, wine farm, town or city.

Qualifications

Qualifications for tourist guides are governed by the National Qualifications Framework (NQF).

There are only two qualifications registered on the NQF:
1. National Certificate in Tourism: Guiding (NQF2)
2. National Certificate in Tourism: Guiding (NQF4)

Several unit standards, within the different areas of specialisation, have been clustered together to form skills programmes addressing areas of specialization, and aimed at persons wishing only to complete the specialized minimum area of learning required to guide.

These skills programmes are registered by CATHSSETA (The Culture Arts, Tourism, Hospitality and Sport Sector Education and Training Authority) for certification purposes. The applicable unit standards are registered on the NQF. In order to register as a site guide specialising in culture, nature, or adventure guiding you need different combinations of unit standards. These rules of combination can be accessed on the CATHSSETA website, at *www.cathsseta.org.za*

To register as a provincial or national guide you need, as a minimum, qualification at NQF level 4 plus the required unit standard for your area of specialization – You can also view these on the CATHSSETA website as given above. Note that the requirements for guide registration, including what learning programme or course is needed for which category of guiding, is the competence of the Provincial Registrars of Tourist Guides.

Tourist Guiding Training and Assessors

All tourist guide trainers and assessors have to be accredited by CATHSSETA to be able to train according to the nationally recognized standards and qualifications network.

Assessors cannot issue certificates as they have to be working for/with an accredited training provider who will then issue certificates from CATHSSETA, upon completion of the assessment. The duration of the course, course content, dates and time of training, fee structure is determined by each training provider.

The guiding qualifications are made up of a collection of unit standards or building blocks. Each unit standard represents knowledge that a person must have, specific to his profession. These unit standards were devised in close consultation with tourist guides and other stakeholders. Each guide is assessed against these standards.

Tourist guides are free to choose any training provider or assessor to work with. Details of accredited tourist guide training providers and assessors are available on the CATHSSETA website at _www.cathsseta. org.za_ or can be obtained by calling their offices on 011 217 0600 or sending an email to _info@cathsseta.org.za_

Recognition of prior learning (RPL) is the type of assessment used for those who have been working as unregistered guides in the past as it takes into account all the qualifications, work experiences, life skills etc. for a particular guide and fits these into the current NQF for guiding. The assessor may point out the areas/unit standards to which extra attention needs to be given. Once the tourist guide has completed this a meeting with the assessor will need to be arranged in order to complete the assessment.

The registration process

No tourist guide may work without being registered.

> NB: CATHSSETA does not register tourist guides. CATHSSETA gives accreditation to training providers so that they can train guides.

According to the Tourism Second Amendment Act no 70 of 2000, any person who wishes to be registered as a tourist guide has to apply to the relevant Provincial Registrar.
In order to be registered as a tourist guide in South Africa, a person must meet the following minimum requirements:
- must be at least 21 years of age;
- must be a South African citizen or be in possession of a valid work permit;
- must have undergone training with a CATHSSETA-accredited training provider;
- must be in possession of a valid first aid certificate from an institution accepted by the Department of Labour;
- submit 4 passport size photos;
- pay a registration fee of R240; and
- must submit a completed and signed registration form and a code of conduct and ethics upon registration.

Proof of registration

The old SATOUR badges and ID cards became null and void on 31 May 2002. Registered tourist guides are now identified by new ID cards which all tourist guides are required to have in their possession whilst guiding. Official tourist guide badges must also be worn whilst guiding. The Provincial Registrar will issue badges and ID cards to new guides only once their application for registering as a tourist guide has been approved. The ID cards indicate the category of guiding, the regions for which the tourist guide was found competent to guide, as well as specialities that the guide might possess. The ID cards are very important because the various policing authorities will request tourist guides to produce these during tourist guide spot checks conducted at various parts of South Africa to identify illegal/unregistered tourist guides.

Renewal of registration

Any person registered as a tourist guide, may before the end of the period for which he/she is registered, apply to the Provincial Registrar for renewal of his or her registration and his/her registration will, upon submission of application forms and other documents and the payment of a prescribed fee, be renewed. _For a full list of Provincial Registrars refer to the table at the end of this article._

Non-compliance

Failure of a tourist guide to complete the NDT registration and CATHSSETA accreditation process but continuing to guide will result in that tourist guide being liable for prosecution. Fines of up to R1 000 can be imposed on illegal guides. Operators found to be using illegal guides can be fined amounts up to R10 000. The process for lodging complaints about unregistered/illegal guides as well as registered/legal guides is outlined in the Second Tourism Amendment Act, 2000. Copies of these can be obtained from NDT offices or from any of the Provincial Registrars' offices.

Tourist Guide Code of Ethics

A Professional Tourist Guide must conform to the Tourist Guide Code of Ethics. The code states that a guide:
- Shall be welcoming and demonstrate an enthusiasm for South Africa.
- Shall at all times show willingness to provide optimum support and quality service to all tourists, and will give tourists an opportunity to enjoy or visit a desired destination.
- Shall in no way discriminate in rendering service to any tourist on any basis, e.g. race, gender, ethnicity, nationality, physical challenge, age, etc.
- Shall be impartial, unbiased and positive, and represent South Africa objectively.
- Shall be suitably dressed and presentable at all times.
- Shall be punctual, reliable, honest, conscientious and tactful at all times.
- Shall be a responsible driver, when driving as a guide.
- Shall carry out the programme/itinerary of a tour to his/her best abilities and be loyal to the company/organization that he/she is representing.
- Shall deal with conflict in a sensitive and responsible manner.
- Shall report any incident of injury or death to a nearby tourist authority or police station.
- Shall be knowledgeable and shall assist tourists and not provide them with misleading information.
- Shall in the event of not being familiar with, or being unable to provide information requested by a tourist, consult with the appropriate authorities for assistance.
- Shall at no time be under the influence of alcohol or a narcotic

substance while on duty and shall refrain from administering any medication to a client without proper medical consultation.

- Shall never solicit for clients or gratuities.
- Shall be concerned at all times for the safety of the tourist.
- Shall wear the appropriate tourist guide badge and will carry his/ her registration card.
- Shall treat all people, cultures and the environment with respect.

How do you find a qualified guide?

The South African Department of Tourism publishes a tourists guide database of qualified guides on its Knowledge Portal website at *https://tkp.tourism.gov.za/touristguide/tgdatabase/Lists/tourguides/ TourGuides.aspx*

Conclusion

Tourist guides are the ambassadors of South Africa's tourism industry. They are often the first, and invariably the last, person that tourists come into contact with and are therefore responsible for creating lasting impressions and fond memories of the country.

This being the case, are tourist guides remunerated in accordance with their importance in the tourism value chain?

Many tourist guides say that they are not, but some Tour Operators argue that a tourist guide's remuneration should be in proportion to his or her experience, qualifications and aptitude.

Information compiled with acknowledgement to Adventure Qualifications Network – www.adventurequalifications.wordpress.com and the South African Department of Tourism: Tourist Guiding.

World Federation of Tourist Guide Associations
2013 Macau Declaration for Tourist Guides Around the World

1. WFTGA declares that its member tourist guides act as ambassadors of their countries and regions and as custodians of their area's traditions, history, culture and environment.

2. WFTGA supports the definition of tourist guiding as an area-specific qualification, usually issued and / or recognised by the appropriate authority. WFTGA believes that any person without a qualification is not competent to interpret and explain the cultural and natural heritage and specialities of that area.

3. WFTGA declares it is not ethical or appropriate for anyone to work as a tourist guide without having the above qualifications.

4. WFTGA declares that tourist guides are essential to the tourism industry and should be acknowledged as professionals by tour operators, tourism stakeholders and local and / or national authorities and be fairly compensated.

5. WFTGA and its member tourist guides stand by our declaration that

" We are the Professionals,"

who work in the best professional manner to achieve high standards of service and contribute to society.

This Declaration was agreed by the WFTGA General Assembly at the 15th International Tourist Guide Convention in Macau SAR China on January 18, 2013.

2013 Macau Declaration

At the World Federation of Tourist Guides Association 15th international Tourist Guide Convention, held recently in Macau, China, the 2013 Macau International Declaration for Tourist Guides Around the World was signed.

South African Provincial Registrars' Contact Details

PROVINCE	AUTHORITY/DEPT	REGISTRAR	TELEPHONE	CELL	FAX	POSTAL	EMAIL
1. Limpopo	Depart of Economic Development, Environment and Tourism	Moses Ngobeni Vukosi Ratshipaladza Stanley Ngwetjana	(015) 293 8510 (015) 293 8504 (015) 293 8538	082 800 2666 082 805 1302 082 771 6240	(015) 291 1085	P/BAG X 9486 POLOKWANE 0700	NgobeniM@ledet.gov.za RatshipaladzaVG@ledet.gov.za NgwetjanaS@ledet.gov.za
2. Mpumalanga	Mpumalanga Tourism and Parks Agency	Musa Mahlangu Justine Hoggan	(013) 759 5328 (013) 759 5477		086 603 6766	P/BAG X 11338 NELSPRUIT, 1200	Musa@mtpa.co.za Justine@mtpa.co.za
3. Gauteng	Gauteng Tourism Authority	Mpho Moeti Pat Naidoo Tsholofelo Mashiane	(011) 085 2101	082 803 1124	086 609 3941	P.O. BOX 155 NEWTOWN 21003	mpho@gauteng.net Pat@gauteng.net tsholofelo@gauteng.net
4. KwaZulu-Natal	Department of Economic Development and Tourism	Peggy Dlamini Sthembiso Zungu	(033) 264 9324 (033) 264 9300	082 952 7575	(033) 264 9316	217 Burger Street Calder Street PMB, 3201	dlaminipe@kznded.gov.za zungust@kznded.gov.za
5. North West	Department of Economic Development and Tourism	Bella Gumede George Masomako	(018) 387 7883 (018) 387 7801	082 674 1788	(018) 387 7886 (018) 387 7924	P/BAG X 15 MMABATHO, 2735	bgumede@nwpg.gov.za gmosomako@nwpg.gov.za lmore@nwpg.gov.za
6. Eastern Cape	Eastern Cape Tourism Board	Thembeka Mbanga	(043) 701 9645 (043) 701 9642	082 771 3462	(043) 701 9600	P.O. BOX 18373 QUIGNEY, 5211	thembeka@ectourism.co.za
7. Western Cape	Department of Economic Development and Tourism	Leigh Pollio (Acting)	(021) 483 9130 (021) 483 2957		(021) 483 8754	P.O. BOX 979 CAPE TOWN, 8000	registrar@pgwc.gov.za lpollio@pgwc.gov.za
8. Northern Cape	Department of Tourism, Environment and Conservation	Andries Mokgele Joy Duze	(053) 830 4875 (053) 830 4881 (053) 831 3530	084 689 7251 079 901 2417	(053) 830 4889	P/BAG X 6102 KIMBERLEY, 8300	amokgele@ncpg.gov.za
9. Free State	Department of Tourism, Environmental and Economic Affairs	Mfundo Ngcangca (Acting)	(051) 400 9598	082 773 8275	(051) 400 9590	P/BAG X 20801 BLOEMFONTEIN 9300	Mfundo@detea.fs.gov.za
National Registry (Pretoria)	National Department of Tourism	Victor Tharage (National Registrar) Uveshnee Pillay Gabriel Dichabe Derick Mbungele Fezeka Monakali	(012) 444 6478 (012) 444 6386 (012) 444 6417 (012) 444 6420 (012) 444 6414			P/BAG X424 PRETORIA 0001	vtharage@tourism.gov.za upillay@tourism.gov.za gdichabe@tourism.gov.za dmbungele@tourism.gov.za fmonakali@tourism.gov.za

Legal

FROM THE BENCH™
With Louis the Lawyer
BENCHMARK ©

RISK IN TOURISM
– PART 17 –
THE LAW: CONTRACTS

REQUISITE #10: ENFORCING YOUR CONTRACT
Homework – What To Do Before You Go Ahead
2. Have The Requisites Been Met? (Continued - 2)

To recap where we ended off in Part 16 last month; The third question is whether there is *consensus ad idem* i.e have the parties actually agreed to the same thing/is there or has there been a *'meeting of the minds'*?

The fourth question that I want to cover here, is whether performance must be possible – we've discussed it in some detail in earlier articles but let's revisit some of the key elements and some new ones.

As mentioned whether or not you are dealing with the impossibility of performance would depend on when that situation arose and whether or not any of the parties were aware thereof: if it existed before the contract is entered into, then of course one of the essentials is missing and there is no contract, <u>BUT</u> there may be a remedy available in delict/tort (more about that later). However if it occurs after the parties have entered into a binding contract then it is a different kettle of fish!

The impossibility of performance may not necessary be due to the fault (negligence or breach of contract) of any party but due to circumstances which may amount to *force majeure*. How that is to be addressed may well be determined by the contract or in lieu of a written contract and/or a *force majeure* clause in the contract, it will be determined by common law.

- *Contractual force majeure* (this is the French version that is strangely a bit wider than the Latin version, which is known as *'Vis Major'*) clauses vary: some mirror the common law whereas others provide for example for the party not affected by the *force majeure* such as the supplier, to retain certain of the funds for administrative fees;

- The <u>common law</u> will mean that there is no obligation/right/duty on either party and matters have to revert to what they were before the force majeure event occurred – take for example the Shingwedzi rest camp in the Kruger National park being devastated by a flood, the adjacent bridge being washed away and all bookings being cancelled (2014).

I also pointed out that it could be even more complex if the contract contained a guarantee or warranty – if this is the case then it does not matter when the impossibility arose. These two terms are often used synonymously, but is it correctly used and what does each word mean?

Guarantee

- A guarantee is <u>usually free</u> and is a promise about an item by the manufacturer or company: product will live up to expectations – is linked to performance of the product after the sale;
- It's a promise to sort out any problems with a product or service within a specific, fixed period of time;
- Normally given by manufacturer;
- Whether you paid for a guarantee or not, it is legally binding;
- The guarantee must explain how you would make a claim in a way that is easy to understand;
- It adds to your rights under consumer law;
- It will take effect whether or not you have a warranty.

Warranty

- A warranty acts like an insurance policy for which you must pay a premium. Sometimes a warranty is called an 'extended guarantee' and refers more to the parts of a product;
- Normally given by retailer or distributor;
- May last longer than a guarantee and cover a wider range of problems;
- A warranty is a legal contract – as opposed to a guarantee, which is mostly part of a contract. A warranty is often a 'stand alone' contract but it is not an implied part of the sale like a guarantee – it is a voluntary optional and additional promise by the provider thereof;
- It is a document issued to protect and extend consumer rights i.e supplier is liable for repair or replacement parts;
- A warranty can be in place with a guarantee.

Finally you have to check whether the contract contains any suspensive conditions and if so, has it/have they been met? The one we are all familiar with is when you purchase a property and then make the sale/purchase conditional upon the buyer obtaining/being granted a bond.

The Global Hotel Industry &
TRENDS FOR
2016

In this latest infographic, Africa and the Middle East are shown to be the most expensive regions for hotel rates with a $165.97 dollar daily room rate on average, writes **Michelle Mangan**.

Did you know that the revenue for the global hotel industry is predicted to rise to $550 billion US dollars in 2016?

The industry as a whole has seen year-on-year increases having been worth $457 billion US dollars in 2011 and $395 billion dollars in 2009. A

s expected, the regions that continue to be key in terms of the highest rates of hotel occupancy are found in Europe and the Asia Pacific regions with both regions filling occupancy at over 68% respectively.

The combined regions of Africa and the Middle East are regions where daily hotel room rates are the most expensive globally. The average room rate in these regions costs $165.97 US dollars per day.

By comparison, the average room rate in the Asia Pacific region costs $115.67 US dollars per day. Considering that its hotel occupancy rates are also so high, this region is one to watch for the rest of 2016.

2016 trends in the hotel industry range from the Millennials replacing Baby Boomers as the dominant consumer group that are spending their time in hotels, to the hotel industry adoption of mobile devices and applications to better service their customers' needs.

These include the needs of the Millennials who crave ultra-personalised services at their fingertips and who are also the most 'connected' generation the industry has ever seen.

The Ard na Sidhe Country House in County Kerry, Ireland, put together this infographic illustrating where the global hotel industry is currently and their predicted trends that are set to dominate the industry this year and into the future.

GLOBAL HOTEL INDUSTRY REVENUE, 2008 TO 2016

- $447 — 2008
- $395 — 2009
- $419 — 2010
- $457 — 2011
- $550 — 2016

Note: Revenue in billions of U.S. dollars.

KEY INSIGHTS »

- The global hotel industry revenue was **$457 billion** dollars in **2011**.
- It is predicted to reach **$550 billion** dollars in **2016**.

HOTEL OCCUPANCY & DAILY ROOM RATES BY REGION

- EUROPE — 68.8% / $138.99
- ASIA PACIFIC — 68.6% / $115.67
- UNITED STATES — 64.5% / $121.37
- MIDDLE EAST & AFRICA — 63.3% / $165.97

% Hotel Occupancy $ Daily Room Rates

Note: Based on 2014 figures

KEY INSIGHTS »

» The occupancy rates in 2014 **increased year-on-year** in **all global regions** suggesting increased demand moving forward into 2016.

» **Europe & Asia Pacific** are **key regions** with the highest occupancy rates.

» The **Middle East & Africa** are the **most expensive regions** for hotel rates.

GLOBAL HOTEL INDUSTRY REVENUE, 2008 TO 2016

$447 — 2008
$395 — 2009
$419 — 2010
$457 — 2011
$550 — 2016

Note: Revenue in billions of U.S. dollars.

KEY INSIGHTS »

The global hotel industry revenue was **$457 billion** dollars in **2011**.

It is predicted to reach **$550 billion** dollars in **2016**.

HOTEL OCCUPANCY & DAILY ROOM RATES BY REGION

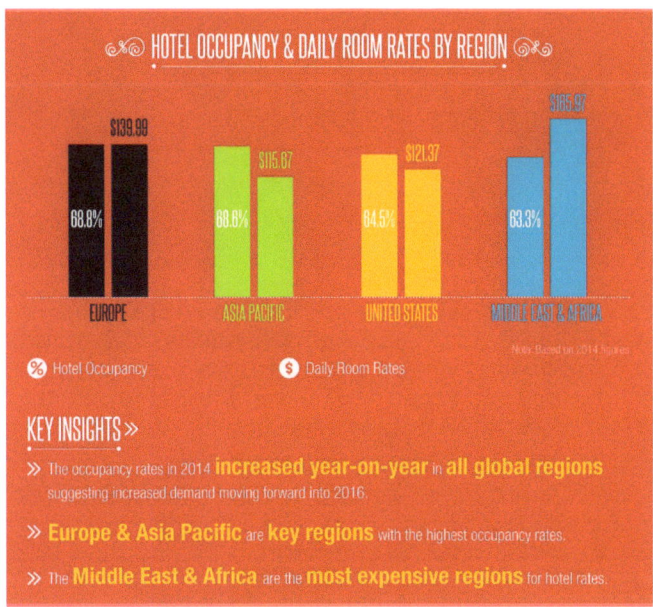

$139.99 — 68.8% — EUROPE
$115.87 — 68.8% — ASIA PACIFIC
$121.37 — 64.5% — UNITED STATES
$185.97 — 63.3% — MIDDLE EAST & AFRICA

Note: Based on 2014 figures.

% Hotel Occupancy $ Daily Room Rates

KEY INSIGHTS »

» The occupancy rates in 2014 **increased year-on-year** in **all global regions** suggesting increased demand moving forward into 2016.

» **Europe & Asia Pacific** are **key regions** with the highest occupancy rates.

» The **Middle East & Africa** are the **most expensive regions** for hotel rates.

PREDICTED HOTEL BUSINESS TRENDS FOR 2016

BUSINESS TRAVEL BECOMES MORE EXPENSIVE IN THE USA

Business travellers in the USA will see the largest **hotel rates** increase in a decade in 2016. Rates are **forecast to rise** from 6.5% to **7.5%**.

MILLENNIALS RISE UP AS THE NEW GLOBAL TRAVELLERS

It is predicted that the **millennial generation** (those between 20-35 years of age) will **replace the baby boomers** as the **dominant consumer** group by 2017.

PREDICTED HOTEL TECHNOLOGY TRENDS FOR 2016

MOBILE DEVICES & APPS WILL ENABLE PERSONALISED GUEST SERVICES

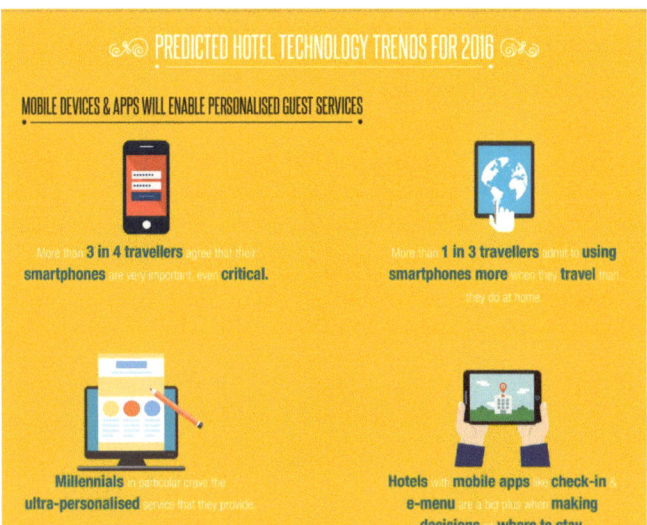

More than **3 in 4 travellers** agree that their **smartphones** are very important, even **critical**.

More than **1 in 3 travellers** admit to using **smartphones more** when they **travel** than they do at home.

Millennials in particular crave the **ultra-personalised** service that they provide.

Hotels with **mobile apps** for **check-in** & **e-menu** are a big plus when **making decisions** on where to stay.

SOFTWARE AS A SERVICE (SAAS) WILL BE THE NEW NORM

Software as a service (SaaS) is a mainstream technology topic in cloud computing, but is a **newer concept** within the **hotel sector**.

Infor, a company that provides advanced software for hotel enterprises, says that **85% of their queries** from **hotels & hospitality** companies are about SaaS.

As hotels become more competitive, they are looking to **cut down** on **operating costs**.

Upfront investment in SaaS is **less expensive** as there are **no initial hardware costs** or **no need for full time IT staff** to maintain the system.

PREDICTED HOTEL MARKETING TRENDS FOR 2016

DYNAMIC RATE MARKETING IN REAL TIME WILL BE STRONGER THAN EVER

More than **50% of hotel bookings** take place **online**.

Increasing a hotel's budget to **chase customers via online channels** can **increase conversions & boost ROI**.

Dynamic rate marketing is commonplace in the world of hotel booking.

This involves **displaying real time pricing & room availability** across a **mix of** online marketing **channels**.

These channels include **display advertising, meta-search, retargeting, Google AdWords, email marketing & Google Business Listings**.

SOCIAL MEDIA ENGAGEMENT IS DRIVING CONSUMER PURCHASING POWER

More than **50% of consumers** worldwide **made a purchase** based on an **online recommendation**.

Social media platforms are now the **main battleground** for hoteliers to **strategically engage** with their **customers** if they wish to grow their room occupancy.

References

www.statista.com/topics/1102/hotels/
ihf.ie/content/six-technology-trends-revolutionising-hospitality-industry
www.statista.com/statistics/247264/total-revenue-of-the-global-hotel-industry/
blog.trginternational.com/3-hospitality-tech-trends-you-dont-want-to-miss-in-2016
www.statista.com/statistics/266741/occupancy-rate-of-hotels-worldwide-by-region/
www.statista.com/statistics/200161/us-annual-accomodation-and-lodging-occupancy-rate/
gogroupbooking.com/the-3-technology-trends-for-hotels-in-2016-you-cant-afford-to-miss/
socialhospitality.com/2015/09/6-hotel-marketing-trends-to-keep-you-ahead-of-the-curve/
skift.com/2015/10/06/u-s-business-travelers-2016-hotel-rates-will-see-largest-increases-in-a-decade/

Ard na Sidhe Country House   www.**ardnasidhe**.com

About the Author:

Michelle Mangan is a Content Marketing Manager who works on behalf of the Ard na Sidhe Country House in County Kerry, Ireland. She frequently researches and creates infographics, storymaps and blogs across a wide variety of topics within the hotel, hospitality, travel and tourism sectors.

For more information visit: www.ardnasidhe.com

Understanding Tourism Trade Insurance
- Part 1 -

We all know that insurance is an essential component of risk management that requires annual review to adjust to changes in the commercial circumstances and legal environment in which we operate. What we may need reminding of are the specific risks that are unique to the tourism trade and need to be considered when mitigating and transferring risk, writes **Des Langkilde**.

The following article will be published in the Tourism Tattler as a series each month, and has been extracted verbatim (with slight editing) from the Southern African Tourism Services Association (SATSA) Insurance Directive booklet with acknowledgement to SATSA and the sponsor of the booklet, SATIB Insurance Brokers, in whose employ I originally re-wrote the text in 2005 and updated in 2015.

INTRODUCTION

Insurance is an emotive issue and viewed by most as a 'grudge purchase'. No-one likes paying insurance premiums for something that may or may not occur but it just might happen to your company and you owe it not only to yourself and your clients, but more importantly to the tourism industry at large, to be adequately insured and fully aware of the procedures in the event of an accident or a claim.

The SATSA Insurance Directive is intended as a general guide for companies operating in the tourism field within Southern Africa. It is directed to all companies undertaking tours, offering accommodation of any nature, those providing an auxiliary activity, and operating or hiring out any form of transport whatsoever.

It is not the intention of this Directive to frighten anyone, in fact quite the contrary. It aims to put forward a realistic set of parameters that apply to Southern African conditions and circumstances and is not based on threats and prohibitive laws that may govern other countries. As a professional tourism service provider you live, work and operate in Southern Africa and it is imperative that it is the tourism industry itself that set the guidelines by which you are prepared and in fact able to function. Obviously these must be based on world norms and the industry must aspire to first world standards.

EC DIRECTIVE

The European Community Directive 90/314/EEC relating to the Package Holidays and Travel Trade Act, 1995 is legislation that governs the conduct of Tour Organisers operating from within European Community member states.

The Act seeks to protect the consumer by making the Tour Organiser liable for the proper performance of the whole tour package, even if the failure or improper performance is due to the fault of a supplier outside of the EC of one or more of the services provided.

If a tourist books a safari holiday in South Africa through an organiser in the UK and is injured at a Game Lodge in South Africa, he need only prove that the Lodge was liable for the injury in order to succeed in a claim against the organiser. Thus, the UK tour organiser is held legally liable for an incident where there is no 'fault' on their part.

In light of this *'liability assumed by contract'* ruling, tour organisers in the EC member states are very cautious in their dealings with Southern African tourism service providers and will want reassurance that the service provider's liability insurance will respond to valid claims and extends to cover the service provider's sub-contractors.

In effect, the local tourism service provider would need to ensure that their liability insurance policy wording extends to cover the EC Directive as 'liability assumed by contract' would generally be excluded in most insurance policy wordings, unless specifically requested.

RISK MANAGEMENT

The first thing to understand about risk is that it is part of our everyday lives.

"Risk is universal, present in all things, all lives, inherent in being. The concept of a person free from risk is as theoretical as the concept of perfection" (Jawarharlal Nehru – 1889-1964).

Given that risk is inherent in being, the question is not so much about how to avoid risk as it is about how to minimise the consequences of risk occurrence, from both a financial and reputation point of view.

Consider these three basic theoretical principles:

- Whenever an event results in the loss of tourist lives (especially international tourists), the global media are almost certain to report it, forcing the local tourism industry to be embroiled in acts of crisis management.

- Perceptions about a particular tourism related crisis tend to be almost as devastating as the crisis itself.

- The farther away one is from a crisis location, the worse the crisis will appear to be and the longer the crisis will remain in the collective travel subconscious.

These principles highlight the need for responsible risk management procedures in every aspect of the tourism industry, from transport to attractions, from hotels to conferences.

What is important for tourism stakeholders to understand is that it is significantly less expensive to manage a risk prior to the event than to deal with a crisis after it has occurred.

LEGAL ISSUES

The concept of a legal duty is a device that law courts (in South Africa specifically) use to determine whether or not it is reasonable to impose liability. A tour operator has a duty to conform to reasonable standards of care. The test of ascertaining the existence of a duty of care in any particular case is the *'foresight of a reasonable person'*. This means that one owes a <u>duty of care</u> to persons to whom harm may be reasonably foreseeable.

In this regard the following questions must be asked:

- Would a reasonable person, in the position of the defendant, have foreseen the possibility of his or her conduct injuring another; and

- Would a reasonable person have taken steps to guard against this danger?

- If so, did the defendant take the steps in question? If not, the defendant would probably be considered negligent.

In the tourism industry, most claims that give rise to liability are personal injury claims. It is also possible for a liability to arise under circumstances where no first aid is available or no proper evacuation plan is in existence.

THE SIZE OF A PERSONAL INJURY CLAIM

A personal injury claim can range from between 5,000 ZAR for a minor whiplash injury to several million for one that results in a victim becoming a quadriplegic. Bearing in mind that the tourism industry attracts high net worth individuals, personal injury claims have the potential to be substantial. It is not uncommon for an injury claim to far exceed the operator's insurance cover limits, which can ultimately lead to the relevant employee of the tour operator being declared insolvent and his or her employer (the tour operator company) being liquidated.

> **Case Study:** *While on a game drive at a private nature reserve in Namibia, the driver lost control of the vehicle, which subsequently rolled. One passenger sustained life-changing injuries while two others were seriously injured. These three guests sued the driver and the safari lodge as the owner of the vehicle. The guest with life-changing injuries was awarded a settlement of $80 (NAD) million and the two other guests were awarded 2.9 million (ZAR) and 3.5 (ZAR) million respectively. Legal fees incurred in defending the case amounted to $10 (NAD) million, with a combined claim value of $96.4 (NAD)million.*

QUANTIFYING RISK EXPOSURE

Compiling a detailed list of all potential hazards within your tourism service that could give rise to potential public liability risks / incidents would be a first step. After carefully implementing procedures and practical measures to minimise each hazard, one should then attempt to quantify, in financial terms, those risks that are unavoidable in order to decide on which would be sustainable using internal resources and which risk exposures would need to be insured.

THE CONCEPT OF INSURANCE

Insurance is a means of transferring risk. In other words, it is a means of covering those risks that are sufficiently large in financial terms that if they occurred, the consequences could cripple your business. Insurance is therefore undertaken not for profit, but to place you in the same financial position as you were immediately prior to the loss.

The objective should be to compile and manage a risk portfolio with minimal exposure, thus ensuring that insurance premiums paid over a period of time accumulate to your benefit by virtue of incentives (no-claim bonuses) being accumulated on an annual basis. Thus a much higher level of exposure and indemnity limit is obtainable at vastly reduced premiums when compared to premiums required for the same level of cover.

TYPES OF INSURANCE

Basically there are 5 kinds of insurance that apply to the tourism industry, and will be covered in this series of articles:

1. Financial Guarantee (Insurance Bond)

2. Liability Insurance

3. Vehicle / Property Insurance

4. Travel Insurance / Medical Rescue

5. Other Business Insurance (Buy & Sell, Key Person, Provident Fund)

1. Financial Guarantee

A financial guarantee, (also referred to as a contingency policy or indemnity bond) is a non-cancellable insurance policy that is created to offset losses arising from specific financial transactions. It is common practice for tourism service providers to ask their clients for upfront deposits to secure travel or accommodation bookings.

A financial guarantee protects the tourists' deposit in the event of the insured service providers' involuntary liquidation. It is important to note that this type of insurance cover will not respond to claims for the reimbursement of deposits where the insured entity has voluntarily gone out of business.

> **TIP:** *SATSA Bonded – SATSA has a contingency policy in place to cover clients as result of a member being placed under involuntary liquidation. Join SATSA to obtain this insurance cover www.satsa.com*

This article will be continued in the February 2016 edition of the Tourism Tattler – Editor.